Mary J. Blige

by Z.B. Hill

Superstars of Hip-Hop

Alicia Keys

Beyoncé

Black Eyed Peas

Ciara

Dr. Dre

Drake

Eminem

50 Cent

Flo Rida

Hip Hop:
A Short History

Jay-Z

Kanye West

Lil Wayne

LL Cool J

Ludacris

Mary J. Blige

Notorious B.I.G.

Rihanna

Sean "Diddy" Combs

Snoop Dogg

T.I.

T-Pain

Timbaland

Tupac

Usher

Mary J. Blige

by Z.B. Hill

Mason Crest

Mary J. Blige

Mason Crest
370 Reed Road
Broomall, Pennsylvania 19008
www.masoncrest.com

Printed and bound in the United States of America.

First printing
9 8 7 6 5 4 3 2 1

Library of Congress Cataloging-in-Publication Data

Hill, Z. B.
  Mary J. Blige / Z.B. Hill.
      p. cm. – (Superstars of hip-hop)
  Includes index.
  ISBN 978-1-4222-2512-7 (hard cover) – ISBN 978-1-4222-2508-0 (series hardcover) – ISBN 978-1-4222-9214-3 (ebook)
 1. Blige, Mary J.–Juvenile literature. 2. Rap musicians–United States–Biography–Juvenile literature. I. Title.
  ML3930.B585H55 2012
  782.421643092–dc23
  [B]
                              2011019651

Produced by Harding House Publishing Services, Inc.
www.hardinghousepages.com
Interior Design by MK Bassett-Harvey.
Cover design by Torque Advertising & Design.

Publisher's notes:
• All quotations in this book come from original sources and contain the spelling and grammatical inconsistencies of the original text.
• The Web sites mentioned in this book were active at the time of publication. The publisher is not responsible for Web sites that have changed their addresses or discontinued operation since the date of publication. The publisher will review and update the Web site addresses each time the book is reprinted.

DISCLAIMER: The following story has been thoroughly researched, and to the best of our knowledge, represents a true story. While every possible effort has been made to ensure accuracy, the publisher will not assume liability for damages caused by inaccuracies in the data, and makes no warranty on the accuracy of the information contained herein. This story has not been authorized nor endorsed by Mary J. Blige.

Contents

Hip-Hop lingo

The Grammy Awards (short for Gramophone Awards)—or **Grammys**—are given out each year by the National Academy of Recording Arts and Sciences to people who have done something really big in the music industry.

An **album** is a group of songs collected together on a CD.

Jazz is a kind of music that began in America. As they play, jazz musicians make up musical patterns around a basic tune. Jazz has a strong rhythm that can change throughout the song.

African Americans started **soul** music by combining the gospel music they sang in church with rhythm and blues. Soul music has a strong rhythm. It's the kind of music that makes you feel like clapping your hands or dancing.

Rap is a kind of music where rhymes are chanted, often with music in the background. When people rap, they make up these rhymes, sometimes off the top of their heads.

If you have **confidence**, you believe in yourself and are sure you can do something.

Chapter 1

The Queen Looks Back

Mary J. Blige stood on a dark stage. At her side, rock band U2 began to play. The first few notes of their hit "One" moved over the crowd. It was the 2006 **Grammys**—and Mary was the star of the night.

Mary was onstage with one of the biggest bands in the world. She began to sing. "One" is about people helping each other. It's a song about what people can do when they work together. Mary knew what it was like to need help. She had come through hard times. She put everything she had into singing "One" that night at the Grammys.

Mary was up for more awards than any artist that night. She had a chance to win eight awards. Mary's **album** *The Breakthrough* was a huge success. Mary had come a long way in her life. She'd dealt with deep pain. She'd been sad for a lot of her life. Things were different now. Mary was happy. She was a star. It was her night.

Mary had become the musician she always wanted to be. She'd become a better person, too. She was married to a good man. She was making music she loved.

Mary was known as the "Queen of Hip-Hop Soul." But growing up, Mary's life was far from royal. Though her life was going well, Mary hadn't always been so happy.

A Queen Is Born

Mary J. Blige was born on January 11, 1971. She was born in Yonkers, New York. Yonkers is just outside of the Bronx, near New York City. Mary's mom was named Cora. Her father was named Thomas. Mary had an older sister named Latonya.

Mary's dad, Thomas, was a **jazz** musician. Before Mary turned four, Thomas left the family. After Thomas left, Cora took her daughters to live in Georgia. Soon, though, Cora was ready to move back to Yonkers.

In Yonkers, Mary lived with her mother, sister, two aunts, and five cousins. Life was hard for Mary and her family. They lived in the Schlobam Housing Projects. Schlobam wasn't a nice place to live. Drugs and crime were a part of life in Schlobam. Many people called the projects "Slow Bam."

When she grew up, Mary said about her life in Schlobam, "Every day I would be getting into fights." Mary said she had to act tough. She had to fight to make sure no one would bother her. Mary told Oprah Winfrey that she'd been sexually attacked in Yonkers when she was young.

Soon, Mary needed a way to escape. She turned to music. She always knew music was there for her. No matter how bad things in Schlobam got, Mary had music.

Mary sang in her church's choir, along with her mother and sister. Then, when she was seven, Mary entered a talent contest. She sang "Respect" by Aretha Franklin and won the contest. Mary decided then that she wanted to be a singer. She had a long way to go before she got there!

Music was Mary's outlet during a difficult childhood. When she was just seven, she won a talent contest singing "Respect," by the legendary Aretha Franklin. In 2001, Mary had the chance to perform with the music diva.

Mary's mom had to work long hours. Cora couldn't always be home for her daughters. Latonya had to be the mother in Mary's house.

Latonya had to iron clothes. She had to do the cooking. She even spanked Mary if she wasn't being good. Mary and Latonya had to grow up fast. They had to take care of themselves.

The rest of Mary's family wasn't much help. Mary's aunts could be mean. They said Mary wouldn't finish high school. They said she'd never do anything with her life. They thought Mary would get into trouble. Even when Mary did well, they didn't act proud of her.

It seemed like everything was against Mary. She felt like she couldn't get away from her family or her neighborhood.

Life didn't get easier for Mary as she grew up. When she was a teenager, she started using drugs. Mary wanted to escape from her life. She turned to drugs to help her deal with her pain.

Mary dropped out of high school in the eleventh grade. She hung out with people who were bringing her down. Mary even got into a knife fight. She still has a scar on her face from that fight. Mary's friends were rough, and so was she.

Mary's life wasn't all fighting, though. She worked some, too. Mary was a babysitter and hairdresser for a while. She also worked as a telephone operator.

But Mary was having a hard time. She didn't want her aunts to be right about her. She wanted to do more with her life. She just didn't know how.

No matter how hard things got, Mary still loved music. Music had helped her get through. She could always count on it. Music let Mary feel good about herself. When she sang, Mary could get her emotions out. She could be herself.

Mary listened to lots of different music. Her mom liked **soul** music. Singers like Gladys Knight and Otis Redding were her favorites. Mary loved soul, too. But she also liked hip-hop.

Hip-hop was born about the same time as Mary. While Mary lived in Yonkers, hip-hop was coming up in the Bronx. Life was hard for many people in New York City at that time. Lots of people were poor. There weren't many jobs. Young people in New York needed a way to express themselves. Like Mary, when times were hard, they turned to music. Rapping let them talk about their lives. You didn't need money to **rap**, either. You just needed a beat and a quick mind. Rap was art anyone could make. Hip-hop gave many young people a voice.

For Mary, hip-hop gave her **confidence**. When she felt bad about herself, hip-hop was there. It didn't make her feel like she was worthless. Hip-hop never told her she couldn't do something. Music was always there for Mary.

Hip-Hop lingo

A **record label** is a company that produces music and sells CDs.

R&B stands for "rhythm and blues." It's a kind of music that African Americans made popular in the 1940s. It has a very strong beat. Today, it's a style of music that's a lot like hip-hop.

A **contract** is a written agreement between two people. Once you've signed a contract, it's against the law to break it. When a musician signs a contract with a music company, the musician promises to give all her music to that company for them to produce as CDs and then sell—and the music company promises to pay the musician a certain amount of money. Usually, a contract is for a certain period of time.

The **hook** of a song is a short section that catches people's attention. A lot of times, the hook is the chorus, but not always.

A **producer** is a person who makes decisions about how an album is made.

Billboard Is a magazine that keeps track of which songs are most popular.

The **charts** are lists of the best-selling songs and albums for a week.

Pop is short for "popular." Pop music is usually light and happy, with a good beat.

Singles are songs that are sold by themselves.

Remixes are new versions of songs that have already been on an earlier CD.

Chapter 2

Pain and Soul

One day when Mary was seventeen, she was hanging out with friends at the mall. Just for fun, Mary sang a song at a recording booth. She recorded Anita Baker's song "Caught Up in the Rapture." Mary didn't think much about it. She liked to sing, that was all.

Her mom, Cora, thought Mary sounded great, though. Cora knew Mary had talent. Cora gave the tape to her boyfriend. He knew someone who worked at a **record label**.

An Open Door

Cora's boyfriend gave the tape to Jeff Redd. Jeff worked at Uptown Records. Jeff sent the tape to the company's president. His name was Andre Harrell.

At that time, Uptown Records was new. They had a few rappers and **R&B** artists. But they were still starting out. When Andre Harrell heard Mary's tape, he knew she was special. He heard the emotion in her voice. He heard her pain. Her voice had soul. He knew he wanted her to sign a **contract** with his company.

In 1989, Uptown Records' president Andre Harrell signed the young Mary to her first recording contract. Though it took a while, this was the beginning of Mary's path to success and out of the desperate conditions of her childhood.

In 1989, Mary met Andre Harrell in person. Harrell signed Mary to Uptown Records right away. She was the youngest artist on Uptown Records. Mary was also the first female artist on the label.

Life didn't change much for Mary, though. The label wanted to focus on working with other artists. Two years went by. Mary sang the **hook** on a song called "I'll Do 4 U" by Father MC. She also got to be in the music video. But Mary wasn't getting the chances she wanted. She wanted to make her own music. She wanted to share her own feelings.

Mary didn't know it, but a door had opened for her. It wouldn't be long before she did get her chance. Soon, Mary would be singing for the world to hear.

What's the 411?

In early 1992, Uptown told Mary to start making her first album. Mary called the album *What's the 411?* She got the title from working as a telephone operator. 411 was the number people called to get information from the operator.

Andre Harrell had Mary work with a new **producer**. His name was Sean "Puffy" Combs. Mary worked with many other people on the album, too. One of them was a man named DeVante Swing.

Swing was a part of Jodeci, an R&B group with Uptown. Swing introduced Mary to K-Ci Hailey, another member of Jodeci. Mary and K-Ci started dated soon after meeting.

Mary's relationship with K-Ci was hard. There were lots of ups and downs. There were good times and bad. Mary loved K-Ci, but he wasn't always good for her.

What's the 411? came out on July 18, 1992. Mary's song "You Remind Me" started playing on the radio that summer. It was a hit! It reached number one on the ***Billboard*** R&B **charts**.

Later that year, another song, "Real Love," hit number one on the R&B charts. It also reached number seven on the Top-10 **pop** songs chart.

The Queen is Crowned

Mary kept putting out **singles** in 1993. By the end of the year, *What's the 411?* had sold three million copies. People started calling Mary "The Queen of Hip-Hop Soul." Mary from Yonkers had become the Queen.

For Mary's first album, *What's the 411?*, she worked with one of the up-and-comers of the music world, Sean "Puffy" Combs. The title refers to Mary's former career as a directory assistance operator. The album's success earned her the title "Queen of Hip-Hop Soul."

My Life was all Mary, her pain, her depression, her honesty. And the fans loved it. She had written most of the songs on the album, and fans let her know they could identify with her music and her pain, a responsibility Mary takes seriously.

Mary released an album of **remixes** in late 1993. It made sure people were hearing *What's the 411?* until 1994. Mary's first album had been a big hit. It was time for Mary's next album.

By that time, Sean Combs had left Uptown Records. He had changed his nickname to Puff Daddy. Combs had also started his own label, Bad Boy Entertainment. Puff Daddy would produce Mary's next album.

Mary and Combs started work on the album. Mary called it *My Life*. This album was different than *What's the 411?* The songs were sadder. Mary's voice showed more of her pain.

Mary hadn't written any songs for *What's the 411?* But for *My Life*, she wrote almost all of them. Mary wanted her album to be honest. She wanted to let people know how she really felt.

Mary was still dealing with her feelings from growing up. She still didn't always feel good about herself. She still felt sad sometimes. She still felt angry, too. Mary wanted to put all these feelings into her music. She wanted *My Life* to be about who she really was.

My Life came out in November 1994. Fans loved it. Mary's voice might not have been the best, but she was real. People who listened could hear her feelings. They could tell Mary really meant what she was singing about.

My Life sold three million copies. The album was another huge success for Mary. It was also proof that people knew where she was coming from. Mary's fans could hear themselves in her songs.

Good Times, Bad Times

Mary seemed to have it all. Her music was popular. People respected her talent. She had two hit albums. But all the pain that had been with Mary since she was young was still there.

Mary was trying to deal with her new success. It was hard work being a famous singer. People wanted a lot from Mary.

Meanwhile, Mary's relationship with K-Ci had gotten worse. K-Ci was mean to Mary. She was in pain. Mary began turning to drugs and alcohol to help. She didn't know what else to do.

Instead of dealing with her feelings, Mary let them build. Soon, people started thinking Mary was hard to work with. They thought she was not easy to be around. Mary just put all of her feelings into her music.

In 1995, Mary worked on many different songs. She recorded songs for movie soundtracks and for TV. Mary also recorded a song with Method Man. The song was called "I'll Be There For

You/You're All I Need to Get By." The next year, Mary won her first Grammy for the song.

On Her Own

Mary made her next album without Sean Combs or Andre Harrell. Combs was working with Notorious B.I.G. at the time. Andre Harrell had left Uptown to go to Motown Records. Instead, Mary produced her own album.

Along with a growing music career came love for Mary and K-Ci Hailey (left) of the group Jodeci. Sadly, theirs was an abusive relationship, and Mary often looked for comfort in drugs and alcohol. She got a reputation for being "difficult."

"I'll Be There for You/You're All I Need to Get By," Mary's hit duet with Method Man, brought the singer her first Grammy Award, Best Rap Vocal Performance by a Duo or Group, in February 1996.

Mary also left Uptown Records. They had helped her become a star. But Mary wanted to move on. She signed a new contract with MCA Records.

Mary brought in people she thought would make her music even better. She worked with R. Kelly and Babyface in the studio, and with others as well.

Mary's third album came out in April 1997. Mary called it *Share My World*. The album went to number one on the charts. The album had hit songs on it with rappers Nas and Lil Kim. *Share My World* sold five million copies.

In 1998, *Share My World* won an American Music Award. It was named Best Album—Soul/R&B.

Soon, Mary ended her relationship with K-Ci Hailey. He had never treated her well. She needed to move on.

Mary had come a long way from Yonkers. She was a famous singer now. She'd gotten away from Schlobam Projects. But Mary still had to deal with her feelings of pain and anger. She was still using drugs to get away from her bad feelings.

Mary didn't live in Schlobam anymore. But she wasn't free yet, either.

Hip-Hop lingo

Something that is **classic** is likely to be popular for a long time.
Critics are people who judge artistic works and say what is good and what is bad about them.

Chapter 3

No More Drama

Mary's next album was just called *Mary*. It was an album of older-sounding songs. Many people thought it sounded like soul from the 1970s or 80s. *Mary* was different from Mary's others. It sounded much less like hip-hop.

Aretha Franklin, Lauryn Hill, and other famous musicians helped make *Mary*. Mary wanted an album that had a **classic** feeling.

Mary didn't sell as well as Mary's other albums. It was just too different for many of her fans. They liked Mary's rougher, more hip-hop sound. When it was released in August, it only went to number two on the charts.

Still, lots of songs on the album were big hits on the radio. MCA Records had an idea for how to get more people to hear *Mary*. They took some of the songs from the album and remixed them. MCA sent the remixed songs to clubs around the country. People who didn't listen to Mary were dancing to her music.

Mary was too honest and not honest enough. She couldn't win. She yelled at people, skipped interviews. Some began to believe that was the *real* Mary J. Blige. She knew better, and she worked hard to change others' opinions about her, and hers about herself.

A remixed "Your Child" even hit number one on the dance charts.

Another version of *Mary* came out at the end of 1999. It was a double album, released as two CDs. The first was the original *Mary*. The second had videos of some of the album's songs. The double album also had a few songs that weren't on the first CD.

After 1999, Mary knew she needed a change. She'd moved past K-Ci. But she was still using drugs. She was still not respecting herself. She was still hard to work with. She needed to change, both for herself and for her music.

Lots of Mary's fans knew what she was going through. Mary's pain was something they also felt. They felt angry and trapped, just like she did. They knew that Mary had troubles like any other person. She wasn't better than anybody just because she was a singer. Her life hadn't been easy just because of her fame.

But in 2000, Mary started to change her life. She started dating Martin Kendu Issacs. He was a businessman at a record company.

Mary also stopped using drugs and alcohol. At first, she turned to food instead of drugs. Soon, though, she knew she had to get in shape. She started to exercise and eat better.

Mary wanted to feel good about herself. She wanted to be healthy. More than anything, Mary wanted to be happy.

Mary's new boyfriend, Kendu, was very nice to her. He helped Mary to quit drinking and using drugs. Mary was respecting herself more. She was learning to deal with the feelings she'd kept inside for so long.

No More Drama

In the summer of 2001, Mary put out a new album. It was called *No More Drama*. The album was Mary's fifth. *No More Drama* was about how much Mary's life had changed. She was finally becoming the person she wanted to be. She was finally learning to be happy.

The first single from *No More Drama* was called "Family Affair." It became the number-one song in the country. The song stayed at

In 2000, Mary took control of Mary. With the help of record executive Martin Kendu Issacs, she kicked abusive relationships, drugs, and alcohol. With two awards at the *Soul Train* Music Awards, including Female Entertainer of the Year, her career was also on the rebound.

number one for six weeks. After that, Mary had another hit with "No More Drama."

At first, No More Drama didn't sell as well as MCA wanted. To change that, MCA put the album on sale again early in 2002. Then, No More Drama started to sell lots more copies. Soon, more than four million copies had been sold.

That year, Mary also won a Grammy. She won for Best Female R&B Vocal Performance for "He Think I Don't Know."

No More Drama was a big change for Mary. The album was happier. Mary wasn't singing about her anger or pain anymore. Her life was changing, and she wanted to share that with her fans. She wanted to show others they could change, too.

Love & Life

In August 2003, Mary released Love & Life. Mary had help on the album from Sean "P. Diddy" Combs. It was the first time they'd worked together since Mary's early work.

Working with P. Diddy was hard for Mary, though. The two didn't always agree on what Mary's music should sound like. Combs wanted Mary to make music that people could dance to. Mary wanted to make the kind of music she knew her fans liked. She wanted to make songs about how she really felt, not parties and dancing.

Love & Life sold well for Mary. Fans and **critics** knew it wasn't Mary's best work, though. Mary knew it, too. She knew she needed to be true to herself. Mary needed to be Mary, not what someone else wanted.

In December 2003, Mary and Kendu were married. Mary felt she'd finally found someone who really loved her. Kendu respected Mary. He always gave her support.

In 2003 Mary and Kendu Isaacs, the man she credits with helping her overcome her self-destructive behavior, were married. She was attracted by his relationships with his family and with God. Mary wanted that kind of life as well.

Mary says that Kendu helped her to make her life better. Kendu's life was about love. He loved his family, and they loved him. Mary knew she wanted to share in Kendu's life. Mary loved Kendu's focus on faith and family.

Mary's life had been full of ups and downs. She knew that *Love & Life* wasn't her best work. She knew she could do better. But she also knew that for the first time, she was happy. Mary was finally happy to be herself. She was finally able to move on from her past. With Kendu at her side and her mind clear, she could do anything.

Hip-Hop lingo

A **victim** is a person who suffers, usually at the hands of another person.
A **victor** is the winner.
A **duet** is a song performed by two people.

Chapter 4

Breakthrough

After *Love & Life*, fans weren't sure what to make of Mary's music. Some didn't know if they liked Mary being happy. They had liked Mary's sad, angry music. But Mary knew she had to be true to herself. She had to put what she felt into her music. She was finally happy, so her music was happier.

Mary knew she had to come back with something real. She needed to show people who she was again. The new, happy Mary was ready for the world.

Mary told one newspaper, "I'm sick of being a **victim**. That's over. I'm the **victor** now."

With that new way of thinking, Mary started working on *The Breakthrough*. It was Mary's seventh album.

The Breakthrough was released in December 2005. In its first week out, the album sold 727,000 copies. It was the number-one album in the country, too.

The Breakthrough ended up selling around seven million copies around the world. It was Mary's best-selling album.

The first single from *The Breakthrough* was called "Be Without You." It was the number-one R&B song in the country for fifteen weeks. The song is still one of Mary's biggest hits.

Mary also had the chance to work with the rock band U2. She recorded their song "One" as a **duet** with U2's singer, Bono. Mary's style fit well with the themes of the song. "One" is about coming

Mary was back on top of things with the December 2005 release of *Breakthrough*. In January 2006, she was ready to sign copies of her CD for the fans who had stood by her through it all.

One of the biggest surprises on *The Breakthrough* was Mary's duet with Bono on U2's megahit "One." In 2006, Mary, Bono, and U2 wowed the crowd when they performed the song at the 48th Annual Grammy Awards.

through hard times with help from others. It's a song about succeeding together.

Mary had changed her life and kept her music real. She didn't need to be sad to make good music. She just needed to be honest. *The Breakthrough* was a big step for Mary. It was proof Mary's best music came from her heart.

Mary also moved on from her past. She understood that the things that had happened when she was young were why she was so sad and angry. Her family hadn't given her support or love. Mary never learned to love herself. Finally, all that was changing.

In 2006, Mary worked on a song with Ludacris. The song, "Runaway Love," was put out on Ludacris's *Release Therapy* album. Mary also worked on a gospel song for the soundtrack of the movie *Bobby*.

In December, Mary put out an album called *Reflections—A Retrospective*. The album had many of Mary's biggest hits. It also had a few new songs. *Reflections* sold 176,000 copies in its first week out.

2007 was a big year for Mary. In February, Mary got to sing "One" with U2 at the Grammys. That night she won three Grammys. She won R&B Song of the Year for "Be Without You." She also won R&B Album of the Year. *The Breakthrough* had taken Mary to the very top.

Growing Pains

Mary's life had turned around. She had made the change she needed. But how could she keep it going? Mary wanted to keep the feeling of *The Breakthrough* alive.

Mary's next album was about that feeling. She didn't want to go back to where she had been. Or to the person she used to be. She wanted to move forward.

Mary called her album *Growing Pains*. She said the name was about taking the bad with the good. It was about making changes for the better. Sometimes, it can be hard to make a change. Mary knew that growing can be hard work!

Growing Pains came out in December 2007. It became the number-one R&B album in the country. The first single from *Growing Pains* was called "Just Fine." It was another hit for Mary. The song was near the top of the R&B and pop song charts.

At the 2008 Grammys, Mary won another award. She won a Grammy for "Disrespectful," a song she sang with Chaka Khan. Mary wrote the song, too.

That year, Mary toured with rapper Jay-Z. They called their tour the Heart of the City Tour. Both Mary and Jay-Z come from New York. Both were also at the top of the music world. They'd been making music for years.

In February 2009, Mary won the Grammy for Best Contemporary R&B Album for *Growing Pains*. The album had been another great success. Even better, Mary was still happy. She was able to keep the feeling of *The Breakthrough*. Her music and her life were both going the way she wanted.

Hip-Hop lingo

A **soundtrack** is a collection of all the songs on a movie.

Charity is money or other help given to those who are in need, doing something to help make their lives better.

A **scholarship** is money given to pay for a student's education.

If you **inspire** people, you make them want to do something and make them feel good about themselves.

Chapter 5

Journey of Love

The Queen of Hip-Hop Soul was going strong. In December 2009, she released *Stronger with Each Tear*. It was her ninth album. The week it came out, it was the number-one R&B album.

The first single from *Stronger with Each Tear* was called "The One." Rapper Drake is also on the song. Trey Songz helped with another single from the album, "We Got Hood Love."

Stronger with Each Tear didn't sell as well as *Growing Pains* or *The Breakthrough*. In its first week, the album sold around 300,000 copies.

Mary's life didn't slow down any, though. She just kept making more music.

In 2009, Mary recorded a song called "Color." The song came out on the **soundtrack** to the movie *Precious*. The song "Stronger" on *Stronger with Each Tear* also came from a soundtrack. Mary first recorded that song for a movie called *More Than a Game*.

That year, Mary was honored at a BET Honors Ceremony. Anita Baker was one of the singers who talked about Mary's music. Mary had sung Anita's "Caught Up in the Rapture" when she was younger.

She'd recorded it in the mall with her friends. It was what started her singing. Now, Anita Baker was honoring Mary. It was something Mary couldn't have even dreamed about as a girl.

In 2010, Mary got to go on *American Idol*. She was a guest judge on the show and also performed Led Zeppelin's "Stairway to Heaven."

After releasing *Stronger with Each Tear*, Mary started work on her next album. In 2011, she released *My Life II... The Journey Continues. My Life II* features rappers like Lil Wayne and Drake, as well as many other artists. The album sold more than 100,000 copies in its first week.

Mary continues to make music that her fans love. She's also making the music that makes her happy.

Mary has also worked on things outside of music. She is interested in business. In late 2010, Mary released her own sunglasses. She called them Melodies by MJB. Her sunglasses come in many different styles. Mary helped make them look the way she wanted.

Mary has her own perfume, too. She worked with a company called Carol's Daughter. The perfume is called My Life. It's named for Mary's album, *My Life*. The perfume is sold on the Home Shopping Network.

Mary's life had changed in so many ways. She has come so far after dropping out of high school. But she didn't forget about school. Instead, in 2010, she got her GED. That means Mary went back and finished her high school education on her own. A GED is a certificate that is the same as a high school diploma.

Mary has gotten her life together. She is healthy and happy. The world has given so much to Mary. And she knows it. That's why she also tries to give something back.

Mary could always count on her fans to stand by her, through thick and thin. So she gives back to the world through her many charitable activities, including work with a dental care outreach program, Crest Healthy Smiles.

Mary's Charity

Over the years, Mary has done lots of work to help others. Mary has performed at many **charity** concerts. She's also started her own charity. She knows that success is best when it can be used to help others. Giving back is important to Mary.

In 2008, Mary helped start the Foundation for the Advancement of Women Now (FFAWN). FFAWN's goal is to help women succeed. They work to give **scholarships** to young women so they can go to college. FFAWN believes that school is the best way to find success.

FFAWN also helps young women with low self-esteem. Mary knows what it's like to feel bad about yourself. With FFAWN, Mary wants to help other women make their lives better.

In 2010, Mary went on the Home Shopping Network (HSN) to sell My Life. The perfume sold 60,000 bottles in one day. It beat the sales record for HSN. One dollar from each sale went to FFAWN.

Mary has also sung at many charity concerts. In 2010, she performed at the Hope for Haiti concert. She also sang at the BET's SOS Help for Haiti concert. Mary wanted to do her part to help Haiti after the 2010 earthquake.

Mary helped make a new version of the song "We Are the World." Many artists recorded the song together. It was sold to make money to help Haiti after the earthquake.

Mary has helped out at charity concerts for a long time. Mary performed at the 2002 VH1 Divas concert. VH1 Divas makes money to help save school music classes. Mary performed with Shakira and Whitney Houston. Mary also performed at the Net-Aid concert in 1999. The NetAid concert helped raise money to send young people to school. NetAid also helps poor people around the world.

Mary knows that helping others is really important. She's had times in her life she needed help, too. Her work with FFAWN and charity concerts is her way of giving back.

An Inspiration to Others

Mary has **inspired** many other artists over the years. When Mary started, her mix of soul and hip-hop was new. Today, many musicians mix these styles the way Mary did. Artists like Alicia Keys, Beyoncé, Keyshia Cole, and many others owe something to Mary. Mary is still inspiring new artists, too.

When she started, people called Mary "the new Aretha Franklin." Today, people might call a new artist "the new Mary J. Blige."

Mary has made it to the top of music. She is still the Queen of Hip-Hop Soul. Almost twenty years after *What's the 411?*, Mary

Despite the tribulations of her life and career, Mary J. Blige has come out a winner. Her music has been groundbreaking, and her inspiration has been important to many who have heard her lyrics and found in them a common bond with the musician.

is still popular. Her music is still helping people get through their problems. Mary's fans still feel as though she is a lot like them.

Mary has had to struggle. Her life hasn't always been good. And you can hear it in her voice. Mary's singing can be sad and beautiful. Her voice can be full of power. But it can also be full of pain.

When fans hear Mary, they feel that struggle. They can hear themselves in the words Mary sings. Her music is from the heart, and fans respect that. Mary is an inspiration to her fans and to other artists.

Looking to the Future

Mary's life has changed a lot since she was young. She's a long way from the Schlobam Housing Projects. She's a long way from the way she felt then, too.

Today, Mary is confident and happy. She respects herself and others. She is married to a man who treats her well. Mary gets to help others with her music and her charity, too. Life has gotten much better for Mary J. Blige.

Mary has made her mark on music. Her style has shown others they can be themselves. Mary has shown how strong she is. By making changes in her life, she helped show others they can change, too. Her music gives support to millions of people around the world.

The future is wide open for Mary. She'll keep making music. She'll keep helping her fans deal with their problems. She'll keep helping other artists make their dreams come true. Mary's going to keep giving back.

Mary's story is about being true to yourself. It's about not letting other people tell you who you are. It's about having the courage to change. And it's about respecting yourself so that others will too.

The Queen is far from done. She's got more to share with the world. And the world is always waiting for more Mary J. Blige.

Time Line

1970s	Hip-hop is born in the Bronx, New York.
1971	Mary J. Blige is born on January 11, in the Bronx.
1989	Signs with Uptown Records.
1992	Releases her debut album, *What's the 411?*
1994	Sean "Puffy" Combs produces *My Life*, Mary's second album.
1995	Covers Aretha Franklin's "(You Make Me Feel Like A) Natural Woman."
1996	Wins her first Grammy.
1998	Wins American Music Award and plays Ola Mae on the *Jamie Foxx Show.*
1999	Records *Mary*, which features Aretha Franklin, Elton John, Eric Clapton, and Lauryn Hill.
2000	Begins relationship with Martin Kendu Isaacs.
2001	Appears in film *Prison Song*.
2002	Performs an emotional rendition of "No More Drama" on the Grammy Awards.
2003	Marries Martin Kendu Isaacs.
2004	Appears in her first off-Broadway play, *The Exonerated.*
2005	Releases critically acclaimed and commercially successful album *The Breakthrough*.
2005	Mary J. Blige lands the title role in MTV's film about Nina Simone.
2006	Appears on the hit television show *Dancing with the Stars.*

2007   In December, *Growing Pains* is released.

2008   Blige tours with Jay-Z and they release a song together, "You're Welcome."

2009   Mary J. Blige performs at President Obama's Inauguration party. She also releases her ninth studio album that December, *Stronger with Each Tear.*

2010   Blige tours for her latest album.

2011   Blige releases *My Life II... The Journey Continues.*

Discography
Albums

1992	What's the 411?
1993	What's the 411? Remix
1994	My Life
1997	Share My World
1998	The Tour
1999	Mary
2001	No More Drama
2002	Dance for Me
2003	Love & Life
2005	The Breakthrough
2007	Growing Pains
2009	Stronger with Each Tear
2011	My Life II... The Journey Continues

In Books

Baker, Soren. *The History of Rap and Hip Hop*. San Diego, Calif.: Lucent, 2006.

Comissiong, Solomon W. F. *How Jamal Discovered Hip-Hop Culture*. New York: Xlibris, 2008.

Cornish, Melanie. *The History of Hip Hop*. New York: Crabtree, 2009.

Czekaj, Jef. *Hip and Hop, Don't Stop!* New York: Hyperion, 2010.

Haskins, Jim. *One Nation Under a Groove: Rap Music and Its Roots*. New York: Jump at the Sun, 2000.

Hatch, Thomas. *A History of Hip-Hop: The Roots of Rap*. Portsmouth, N.H.: Red Bricklearning, 2005.

Websites

Mary J. Blige
www.maryjblige.com

Mary J. Blige
www.starpulse.com/Music/Blige,_Mary_J.

Mary J. Blige on Myspace
http://www.myspace.com/maryjblige

MTV: Mary J. Blige
http://www.mtv.com/music/artist/blige_mary_j/artist.jhtml

Rock on the Net: Mary J. Blige
www.rockonthenet.com/artists-b/maryjblige_main.htm

Index

About the Author

Z.B. Hill is a an author and publicist living in Binghamton, New York. He has a special interest in adolescent education and how music can be used in the classroom.

Picture Credits